AYRSHIRE BUSES

David Devoy

AMBERLEY

First published 2014

Amberley Publishing
The Hill, Stroud
Gloucestershire, GL5 4EP

www.amberley-books.com

Copyright © David Devoy, 2014

The right of David Devoy to be identified as the
Author of this work has been asserted in accordance
with the Copyrights, Designs and Patents Act 1988.

ISBN 978 1 4456 4175 1 (print)
ISBN 978 1 4456 4185 0 (ebook)

British Library Cataloguing in Publication Data.
A catalogue record for this book is available from
the British Library.

Typeset in 9.5pt on 12pt Celeste.
Typesetting by Amberley Publishing.
Printed in the UK.

Introduction

My first introduction to the Ayrshire bus cooperatives was probably as a young child, when my parents used to take my sister and I to visit Ayrshire on days out, often by bus as we had no car at the time. Another chance would be on Sunday school trips to the coast. I was never interested in the games since I was distracted by the never-ending variety of buses that used to drive past on service. No wonder I never won the egg and spoon race! I was so naïve at the time that I thought AA buses were somehow connected with the Automobile Association! Gradually the real picture emerged and I learned the facts over the years, and as I became old enough to visit the area on my own I began to take photographs and have built up a good collection over the years, helped by many other enthusiasts too. Even today, when I feel down in the dumps, I can dig out some slides and many happy memories come flooding back. It was a great loss to the area when all the wonderful liveries faded into history to be replaced by standard Stagecoach colours, which are essentially the same wherever you go in the country. I feel privileged to have known many of the operators over many years and cannot thank them enough for always making me welcome and finding time for a chat. No attempt has been made to separate the fleets depicted as they were all to be seen together in the real world, and it was the rich mixture of colours that complimented one another that gave the area its unique tapestry. By the same token, we go back and forward through the years in no particular order, but that aside I hope you enjoy looking at the pictures, which all come from my own private collection.

There were around sixty small operators running in the Ayr/Kilmarnock/Ardrossan area in the early 1920s, when major company Scottish General Transport began a service linking Ardrossan and Kilmarnock, working to a set timetable. Most of the small operators competed along various parts of the route, but they began to fear for their future when Scottish General moved their headquarters to Kilmarnock in 1924 and began to develop a network of routes throughout Ayrshire. They realised that they would have to work together in order to survive, as none owned enough buses to compete on a set timetable. In 1925 they sent a party to study a bus owners' association that traded in Lanarkshire as A1 Service. They reported back and decided to set up a similar arrangement in Ayrshire the following year. The new association began running co-ordinated services from Ardrossan to Kilmarnock using a set timetable, while a separate association began running local services (LS) between Saltcoats and Stevenston. Around forty bus owners decided to join the new A1, but in the early days members came and went, sometimes being replaced by others.

A breakaway association (Clyde Coast Services) was formed in 1929 by some former A1 and LS members who decided to concentrate on the route from Saltcoats to Largs. In 1930 the remaining members of A1 decided only to compete with Scottish General between Ardrossan and Kilmarnock. This upset some members who wanted to expand and led to more leaving to set up Ayrshire Bus Owners Association (AA Service), working the area between Ardrossan and Ayr. The next year saw the remaining twenty-two members of the A1 and LS cooperatives merge to form a new Ayrshire Bus Owners Association (A1 Service), with all duties shared equally between all members. One share was cancelled without replacement, leaving twenty-one equal shares needing two buses to operate each share. All members were responsible for providing and maintaining their own vehicles and premises. The passing of the 1930 Road Traffic Act forced all the Associations to be set on a more formal footing to ensure the traffic commissioners knew who was responsible for licensing, etc. Things settled down with no drastic changes, although shares were sold from time to time. The early 1950s were a tough time and the A1 company offered itself for sale to Northern Roadways of Glasgow. The offer wasn't taken up and things eased from 1956, when London Transport started selling off modern vehicles at keen prices. This allowed many owners to restock their fleets. A few outsiders bought shares in the 1950s until it was decided that future sales could only be to family relations or other members. Inevitably, as owners retired, too many wanted out in too short a time; no one could afford to buy their shares and eventually the company offered itself to Stagecoach. The takeover occurred in January 1995. The Clyde Coast members were joined by another couple of operators and settled down to a half-hourly service between Saltcoats and Largs, with contracts and private hire under the same banner, until one by one the membership dwindled to only two, and they merged in 1988 and formed Clyde Coast Coaches in 1990, but eventually became more involved in property than coaches and eventually ceased running buses altogether. The service had been purchased by Stagecoach in 1995.

AA Motor Services was formed in 1930 when five members of A1 left to concentrate on the Ardrossan to Ayr service and were quickly joined by another couple of operators. The combined fleet totalled sixteen buses. Further expansion occurred over the years with local services in Irvine added. Eventually, only Dodd's of Troon were left as the others had retired and the services passed to Stagecoach in 1997, although Dodd's continues to operate coaches. A unique way of life had passed into history as the small operators were replaced by a PLC.

AAG 648B was a Daimler Fleetline CRG6LX/Northern Counties H74F, new to AA member Robert Tumilty in July 1964. Robert was based at Gailes Garage in Irvine, which had been acquired from fellow member Robert Watson. When Tumilty retired in September 1972 his share was divided between Young's and Dodd's. This bus went to Dodd's, where it was given a refurbishment that included removing the engine shrouds and a full repaint into Dodd's version of the livery. This shot sees it in Irvine while working a local service in 1978, although it would last a further two years.

LCU 120 was a Daimler CCG6/Roe H63R new to South Shields Corporation in June 1964. It was acquired by A1 Service member Tom Hunter in February 1974 and lasted until 1977. It was caught in Stevenston town centre on its way to New England.

JSD 941F was new in April 1968 to A1 Service member James McKinnon of Kilmarnock. This Leyland Atlantean PDR1/1 had bodywork by Northern Counties of Wigan to a design pioneered by Nottingham Corporation. It ran until February 1982 but was not actually sold until the September, when it passed to Ayrshire operator Kerr of Galston. This view was taken in Ardrossan and the building in the background on the left was the western depot.

EAG 267D was a Leyland Atlantean PDR1/1/Northern Counties H77F built to Nottingham style. It was new to AA member Young's of Ayr in January 1966 and it remained in service until April 1981. Young's were not an original member of AA Motor Services and only joined in 1931, when they acquired the share of Charles Law of Prestwick. For legal reasons some vehicles were licenced to G. Gemmell of Ayr, who was the company accountant. This view from 1978 sees EAG 267D working an Irvine local service, but as the years went by Young's were to be seen less often in Irvine as they swapped some Ayr local workings with Dodd's to cut down on dead mileage. Young's retired from AA in April 1992 and all operations passed to Dodd's of Troon.

KSD 661F was a Leyland Atlantean PDR1A/1/Massey H74F new to A1 Service member Andrew Hunter of Dreghorn in May 1968 and lasted in the fleet until April 1979. It was photographed at the old bus station in Kilmarnock. The upright styling was old-fashioned even when the bus was new, but I must admit I liked it. Massey Bros tended to build for corporations and the likes of Colchester and Maidstone had similar vehicles.

KSD 228P was an AEC Reliance 6MU4R/Duple Dominant B53F new to AA member Dodd's of Troon in November 1975. On disposal it went to Hyster, Irvine (Non PSV), then Irvine's of Law and Stuart's of Carluke. This view was taken in Troon as it headed towards Ardrossan.

SCO 425L was a Leyland National 1151/2R B46D purchased new by Plymouth City Transport as their No. 25 in September 1972. These buses were very unpopular in Plymouth and put up for sale early in their lives. Clyde Coast member Kenny McGregor decided to try the type and purchased two in 1978. SCO 425L arrived in May and would remain in the fleet until August 1982, although it had been converted to B50F in July 1981 using parts from sister RCO 616K. It was used as a seat store after withdrawal and broken up on site around 1985.

EGB 80T was a Leyland National LN11351A/1R B52F new to Central Scottish in December 1978 as their N3. It passed to Western Scottish in 1989 and became L580. It returned to Ayrshire in 1992 to join the fleet of A1 Service member Hill of Stevenson and remained until January 1995, when the fleet was sold to Stagecoach. EUM 889T was a Leyland National LN11351A/1R B49F purchased new by West Riding (59) in April 1979. On disposal in January 1991 it passed to the dealer Lonsdale of Morecambe before reaching AA member Dodd's of Troon in July of that year. It would remain in service until November 1995, when it passed to Delta of Kirkby-in-Ashfield as their 689.

PAG 318H was a Leyland Leopard PSU3A/4R/Plaxton Panorama Elite C51F new to Docherty in 1970. The livery was based on that of Websters of Wigan, a constituent of Smiths-Shearings. Docherty used the fleetname Cosy Ha' on his coaches. This was the depot in Bank Street in Irvine where the coaches shared space with Docherty's A1 Service fleet.

GSJ 963N was a Leyland Leopard PSU3B/4R/Plaxton Elite Express C53F new in 1975. It was a McGregor vehicle, easily identified as the livery proportions were different for Frazer and McGregor's coaches. It was a Leyland Leopard PSU3B/4R/Plaxton Elite C53F delivered new in February 1975 and lasting until December 1989, when it was sold to dealer Joe Sykes of Barnsley. Joe resold it to Stephenson's of Easingwold in October 1990 and it finished its life with the St Helens Angling Club in 1991.

ASD 891B was an AEC Renown/Park Royal H74F purchased new by A1 Service member James McKinnon of Kilmarnock in November 1964. It was travelling down Glasgow Street in Ardrossan on the local route to Stevenston pillar box. It would remain in service until April 1979.

NSJ 380R was a Leyland Fleetline FE30ALR/Alexander H74F purchased new by AA member Dodd's of Troon as their DT23 in August 1976. It is seen in Irvine wearing a version of the livery that featured less cream on the upper deck, but this was later rectified to the normal version.

KVD 13E was an AEC Reliance 6MU3R/Willowbrook B53F new to Lanarkshire independent Hutchison of Overtown in April 1967. It was one of three purchased by Clyde Coast member McGregor of Saltcoats in 1972, but this one only lasted until 1974. It was approaching the junction with Glasgow Street in Ardrossan while working on the Largs service.

ASD 32T was a Volvo Ailsa B55-10 Mk II/Alexander H79F bought new in February 1979 by A1 Service member Thomas Hill, who traded as the Stevenston Motor Company. The Ailsa was built nearby at Irvine and it was good to see local operators supporting local jobs.

Dodd's of Troon maintained a separate coach fleet and KCX 17S was a little Bedford VAS5/Plaxton Supreme C29F purchased second-hand from the Dewhirst Coal & Transport Company in 1979. Dodd's (Coaches) was formed as a separate company from the buses in August 1946 at a time when the Labour government was proposing nationalisation of the county's bus network. In the event it never happened, but it's better not to have all your eggs in the one basket.

Unlike the other companies featured, Clyde Coast Services ran their coach operations alongside the service work and often used the same vehicles. WSD 368K was a Leyland Leopard PSU3B/4R/Plaxton Elite C53F owned by Hugh Frazer of Fairlie. Despite the destination screen being set for Largs, it was actually on a football hire to Glasgow. It was quite common for around a dozen coaches to be on this type of work on a Saturday.

OCS 34X was a Dennis Dominator/East Lancs H76F purchased new by A1 member Ian Duff of Ardrossan in December 1981. His share was operated from Parkhouse Garage in Ardrossan and the family still own the premises, where petrol is sold alongside car repairs. It was running through Irvine when photographed.

SDU 930G was a Daimler Fleetline SRG6-30/Alexander W Type B45D which was new in February 1969 as a demonstrator for Daimler Transport Vehicles Limited. It was originally fitted with a Perkins V8 engine but this had been changed for a Gardner engine before the bus was acquired by AA member Dodd's of Troon in July 1973. The centre doors were removed in August 1980 and the bus later acquired a broadside advert for the associated business of Dodd's TV and Video. It remained in service until June 1984, after which it was dismantled for spares. This view shows it in Irvine on a local service.

Technically, Clyde Coast ceased to be a cooperative after April 1988, when the fleets of McGregor's and Frazer's merged to become a single business. OSJ 627R was a Leyland Leopard PSU3C/3R/Alexander Y Type B53F purchased new by Western SMT as their L2627 in December 1976. It was purchased in August 1997 for use on schools and contracts and is preparing to leave its Ardrossan depot.

HVD 639 is laying over at Parkhouse Bus Stance in Ardrossan on a foul day. It was an all-Leyland Titan PD2/10 new to Lanarkshire independent Hutchison's of Overtown in 1953. It only lasted three years before sale to A1 member Reid of Saltcoats, but survived in Ayrshire long enough to pass to Docherty of Irvine after Reid retired in 1966, and served until 1969.

Nobel Industries Limited was founded in 1870 by Swedish chemist and industrialist Alfred Nobel for the production of the new explosive dynamite. Ardeer, on the coast at Ayrshire, was chosen for the company's first factory. At its peak, the factory was employing nearly 13,000 men and women. This view dates from June 1975, when things were beginning to wane, and we can see vehicles belonging to Western SMT, A1 Service and Clyde Coast Services, and if Alfred Nobel gave a prize for the most interesting bus stations, then surely this would be among the contenders.

PCS 443 was a Leyland Tiger Cub PSUC1/1/Northern Counties B44F delivered new to AA member Robert Tumilty of Irvine in June 1960. It remained in service until August 1971 and was on the Ayr-Stewarton service. The adverts around the bus station are of note. You could buy twenty Kensitas Club cigarettes for 23p. Another delightful touch is the blackboard used for Dodd's coach tours and that day's offering was a tour at 1.30 p.m. to the Trossachs for only 75p or a 2.30 departure covering Barr and Girvan for only 35p. Britain had only gone decimal on 15 February 1971 and Robert Tumilty retired from AA Motor Services in September 1972, when his share was divided between Dodd's and Young's.

Clyde Coast member Hugh Frazer bought KCS 525 in June 1957 and continued to operate it till 1973. It was a Burlingham bodied Leyland Tiger Cub and this 1972 view catches it skirting the coast near South Beach on the half-hourly service linking Saltcoats to Largs.

UCS 896S was a Volvo Ailsa B55-10/Alexander H79F in the fleet of Docherty and was loading in its home town of Irvine. Docherty vehicles often sported a heavy-duty front bumper and this is no exception. Docherty only joined A1 in 1957, when the share of Alistair MacPhail of Irvine was purchased, and just after this a condition was applied to prevent any further outsiders from joining the company as shares could only be passed to members' families or other members.

When production of the Daimler Fleetline was being phased out, Dodd's turned to the Dennis Dominator/East Lancs as a replacement. OCS 727X was the second one purchased new by AA member Dodd's of Troon in January 1982. It would remain in service until August 1991, when it passed to White Rose Coaches of Glasshoughton, then Ashall's of Levenshulme for further service. It was caught passing through Troon while bound for Ayr.

This was the fleet of Hunter's of Crosshouse in July 1979, shortly before a disastrous fire engulfed the premises on the night of 6 December 1979. OAG 761L was parked outside the garage at Crosshouse. In an act of vandalism, it was set on fire and the flames quickly spread to the buildings, which contained other buses. GSD 366, a 1950 Daimler; Daimler Fleetlines CVG6/TAG60/WAG709/OAG761L; and Volvo Ailsas NCS23/4P were totally destroyed. UCS 763 and PAG 760H were badly damaged. The only remaining buses untouched were RAG 578 and ECS 57V. In true A1 fashion, services were maintained by borrowing buses from other members to work the company's share. Even Western helped by supplying LXS 14K and LXS 866L, which had recently been acquired from Cunningham's of Paisley.

OSJ 747R was a Leyland Leopard PSU3C/4/R/Plaxton Elite Express C53F purchased new by Kenny McGregor in November 1976. It shows a further variant of the livery, for around this time the company was striving to modernise its image and make the fleet more appealing to potential customers. This coach was a diverted order from Barton Transport of Nottingham and had been registered as NTO 483P, but this was voided before delivery.

With production of Dodd's previous standard, the AEC Reliance, ending, the company was forced to seek a replacement model. FSD 99V was a Volvo B58-56/Plaxton Supreme C53F, purchased new in February 1980. Although expensive to purchase, it was very reliable in service and many further Volvos have followed over the years. It was sold to Fraser of Munlochy in 1987.

LVS 430P was an AEC Reliance 6U3ZR/Plaxton Supreme C53F purchased new by Limebourne of London in 1976. It was acquired by Duff of Ardrossan in November 1983 for use on the Glasgow service as well as private hire work. It was getting ready to leave from Park's City Independent Coach Terminal in Glasgow and I travelled on it to Ayrshire that day.

TSD 163S was a Leyland Atlantean AN68A/1R/Roe H78F purchased new by J. C. Stewart in November 1977. It is shown as it passes Arran Place in Ardrossan and carries extensive advertising for Stewart's travel agency. It would last in service until May 1992.

AA member William Young of Ayr used a different shade of green on his vehicles. The family had extensive transport interests in Renfrewshire and one of the sons, Andrew Young, moved to Ayr in 1919 to manage the business of John Gemmell Ltd. He bought the business in 1921 and started local bus services in Ayr. Andrew was not an original member of AA, only joining in June 1932, when he purchased the share of Charles Law of Prestwick, although Law later rejoined. A pair of Leylands is seen resting at the company's depot in Carrick Street in Ayr.

XCS 374M was an AEC Reliance 6MU4R/Willowbrook Expressway 002 C51F purchased new by Clyde Coast member McGregor of Saltcoats in July 1972. It was passing through Largs on a dull day and would last until 1980, when it passed to Canavan of Croy.

SCS 204J was a Seddon RU/Pennine B51F purchased new by Dodd's of Troon in January 1971. It was captured in Irvine, looking superb in Dodd's classic version of AA livery. It was withdrawn in 1979 after an accident and dismantled for spares. The Seddon RU featured a Gardner 6HLX engine, which appealed to Dodd's.

LFS 429 was a Leyland Titan PD2/20/Metro-Cammell Orion H60R bought new by Edinburgh Corporation as their 429 in June 1954. It was one of eight similar buses purchased by A1 members in 1970/1, and J. C. Stewart owned this one. It would remain in service until around 1975.

BCS 583T was a Bedford YMT/Willowbrook Spacecar C49F purchased new by Dodd's Coaches in April 1979 and was part of an order cancelled by National Travel. It was visiting Glasgow on a private hire and would run until 1985, when it was sold to Field of Balby.

ASD 891B was an AEC Renown/Park Royal H74F, one of a pair purchased by McKinnon of Kilmarnock in November 1964. McKinnon had purchased the share of Townsley in the 1950s and adopted the white roofs favoured by that firm. Eventually, the other members forced them into line and blue roofs became the norm.

CXS 556D was a Daimler Fleetline CRG6LX/Alexander H78F new to Graham's of Paisley in July 1966. It was one of a pair put into service by Dodd's in November 1979 to cover for accident damage and is seen at Troon with the broadside panels ready for the signwriter to apply an advert. It was withdrawn in 1990 after a low bridge accident and the intention was to convert it to an open-top vehicle, but the project was abandoned.

PAG 766H was a Daimler Fleetline CRG6LX/Alexander D Type H75F purchased new by Duff of Ardrossan in March 1970. It would remain in service for a credible thirteen years and was wearing the full version of the livery, complete with blank advert panels and maroon band.

WCS 830K was a Leyland Atlantean PDR1A/1/Alexander J Type H78F purchased new by A1 Service member Claude Dunn of Stevenston in May 1972. It was withdrawn in May 1982 and joined Clyde Coast member Kenny McGregor's fleet. Its stay was short, however, as it moved on three months later to Smith of Dalmellington. Strangely, it rejoined Clyde Coast in 1989 and was caught at Fairlie Depot.

SSD 636M was another member of Hugh Frazer's fleet and shows the traditional Clyde Coast livery of blue and grey to good effect. It was a Leyland Leopard PSU3B/4R/Plaxton Elite C51F, delivered new in May 1974, and was working on a football hire to Glasgow.

245 AJF was one of three ex-Leicester MCW bodied Leyland Titans bought second-hand by A1 in 1975. It is pursued through Saltcoats by a BMC van of Homepride Bakeries as it heads for Kilmarnock on the main trunk service. It was owned by Claude Dunn from 1975 until 1977. The unusual positioning of the registration plate was a Leicester idiosyncrasy.

It is fair to say that the early models of the Leyland National were not the most reliable of buses, and Plymouth Corporation decided to cut their losses and dispose of the type prematurely. Clyde Coast member Kenny McGregor decided to try the type and purchased two in 1978. SCO 425L arrived in May and would remain in the fleet until August 1982, although it had been converted to B50F in July 1981 using parts from sister RCO 616K. It was running through Largs on the service to Saltcoats.

OSD 178 was not all that it appeared to be, for it was another ex-Plymouth bus which had been new in 1944, registered as CDR 757. It was a Guy Arab II and was purchased by Dodd's in 1954 and stored. It was rebuilt over the next six years before being sent to Northern Counties for new sixty-four-seat bodywork, and remained in service until 1973. It was leaving Dodd's garage in Dundonald Road in Troon to work on a school contract.

GSD 366 leaves the ICI Plant at Ardeer with a good load of factory workers at the end of their shift. It was a Daimler CVG6/Northern Counties H60R, purchased new by Hunter's of Crosshouse in April 1955 and sadly destroyed in a depot fire in December 1979.

NCS 26P was a Leyland Leopard PSU3C/4R/Duple Dominant C51F, bought by Docherty of Irvine primarily for use on the Broomlands Community Route, which linked Irvine and Dreghorn using some bus-only roads in Irvine New Town.

Dodd's didn't neglect their coach operations and continued to invest in new vehicles. MSD 336W was a very smart new Volvo B58-61/Duple Dominant C53F, purchased new in April 1981, which wore a modern version of the traditional livery. It would remain in the fleet for eight years before sale to Palmer of Carlisle.

NSJ 380R was one of a pair of Leyland Fleetline FE30ALR/Alexander H74Fs purchased by Dodd's in August 1976 and was nearing the end of its journey at Arran Place in Ardrossan. Reluctantly, Dodd's had to accept Leyland engines in this pair in order to achieve early delivery, but Gardner engines were later fitted. This bus was involved in a low bridge accident and repaired using the roof from A1 Service OAG 757L in January 1986.

E755 TCS was a Scania K112CRB fitted with Van Hool Alizee C49Ft bodywork and was new in April 1988. It would remain in service until the start of the 1995 season, but was re-registered as TJI 5399. Dodd's re-invested the money from the sale of their bus interests back into the coach business and operate many coach holidays nowadays.

Docherty of Irvine purchased this former demonstration Leyland Atlantean PDR2/1/ Park Royal H47/32D in February 1971 when it was only three years old. It looked really modern at the time and was sitting at Parkhouse bus stance in Ardrossan. It would last until 1983. It fitted in well with the Docherty fleet as two similar vehicles had been purchased new in the preceding couple of years.

Clyde Coast were still trying to adopt a fancier livery when TSJ 678S was given this scheme. It was a Leyland Leopard PSU3E/4R/Plaxton Supreme Express C53F in the McGregor fleet. It had been purchased under the Government's Bus-Grant scheme and had to operate 50 per cent of its mileage on service work.

DWW 433H was a Leyland Leopard PSU3A/4R/Plaxton Derwent B51F body, new to United Services in June 1970. It passed to Black Prince of Morley in January 1982 but was not used. They traded it into Ensign against an ex-Western Leopard. After CCS, it went to Irvine's of Law in August 1985. Note the Leyland National badge, taken from a scrapped ex-Plymouth Leyland National.

OCS 114R was a diverted order from Proctor's of Hanley. It was a Daimler Fleetline CRG6/Alexander H75F, delivered to A1 Service member McKinnon of Kilmarnock in July 1976. It always seemed to look old-fashioned and was bound for Kilmarnock when photographed in Irvine High Street.

Dodd's purchased LSJ 872W in April 1981 and it was crossing the bridge over the River Ayr as it neared the bus station. It was an Leyland National NL116AL11/1R B52F and survived until 1997, when the services passed to Stagecoach, and became Western number 765.

WAG 513K was a Leyland Leopard PSU3B/4R/Plaxton C53F purchased new in December by T. & E. Docherty of Irvine for their Cosy Ha' coach fleet. It later gained A1 Service livery for use on the Glasgow service and was sold to fellow A1 member Meney of Ardrossan in 1986. It was sold to Clyde Coast Services in October 1988 and was spotted in Ardrossan.

NSD 211G was a Leyland Atlantean PDR1A/1/Alexander H45/30D, new to Tom Hunter of Crosshouse in June 1969. It was transferred to son John in 1978, when the operations were split between T. & J. Hunter and John Hunter. This came about as older members retired and sold their stake and it was felt that T. & J. Hunter had too many shares.

Dodd's worked under contract to Scottish Citylink and WSV532 proved to be an unusual choice of vehicle. It had begun life with Trathen's of Yelverton as ADV142Y in 1982. It passed to Townsend-Thoresen Holidays and joined Dodd's fleet when they bought the coaching side of the business in 1986. It was a Volvo B10M-61/Padane C49Ft and was seen in Glasgow's Anderston bus station in May 1988.

H455 WGG was a Scania N113CRB/Alexander PS Type B51F purchased by Dodd's in August 1990 and was laying over at the Ardrossan Terminus. It lasted until the end of AA operations in June 1997 and became Western number 453.

Two immaculate Daimler Fleetline CRG6LX/Alexander D Type H75F deckers are caught side by side at Saltcoats Railway station as the crews exchange greetings. Both belonged to Ian Duff of Ardrossan and were new in 1970 and 1966 respectively. Surely this has to be one of the classic liveries of all time, complete with cream advert panels.

It was normal practice for Clyde Coast to use their older coaches on the service to finish their days. VSD 59 was a Leyland Leopard L2/Plaxton Panorama C43F purchased new by Frazer's of Fairlie in April 1963 and was loading outside the company's office in Saltcoats in June 1975.

Dodd's made extensive use of advertising on their buses and ASJ 206T was certainly eye-catching when seen in Irvine. It was a Leyland Fleetline FE30AGR/Alexander H78F purchased new by AA in April 1979. It passed to Western Buses as fleetnumber 839 in 1997 but was not operated.

As the years went by, it became usual practice for larger batches of new vehicles to be purchased together. In 1973 this meant three Fleetlines and five Atlanteans to this style; OAG 759L was a Daimler Fleetline CRG6LX/Alexander H74F new to James Brown of Dreghorn in May of that year.

M389 KVR was a Dennis Dart/Northern Counties B39F bought new by Dodd's in March 1995. It is shown wearing the later version of the livery with AA Buses titles as it passes through Irvine. It passed to Western Buses with forty other vehicles on 29 June 1997 and an era had passed into history.

A classic scene at Saltcoats Town Centre shows LFS 414, which was operated by Robert Meney from June 1971 till 1973. It had been new to Edinburgh Corporation in June 1954 and was a Leyland Titan PD2/20/Metro-Cammell Orion H60R.

A1 caused considerable surprise when they purchased UGG 920W from Cotter's Glasgow dealership. Member J. C. Stewart operated this Volvo B58-61/Van Hool Alizee C51F from June 1981 until January 1985 on a mixture of work, including travel agency work and the express services to Glasgow. The location was Park's City Coach Terminal in Glasgow, which is where the Royal Concert Hall now stands.

D39 HMT was a Leyland Royal Tiger/Van Hool C53F purchased new by Hugh Frazer in August 1986. It was to be the last Leyland bought new and, sadly, poor reliability and service soured the relationship with Leyland. It only survived until 1988, when it was traded in to a dealer against a new Volvo.

Clyde Coast tried the Leyland Lynx in August 1992 when they borrowed J375 WWK from Volvo Bus and it is seen on the service passing through Largs. It was later purchased by Brewer's of Port Talbot as their fleetnumber 509.

TSD 571S was a Leyland Atlantean AN68A/1R/Northern Counties H78F purchased new by AA member Young's of Ayr in January 1978. It was passing South Beach as it headed back to Ayr and carried the later AA Buses fleetname, first introduced in 1984. On disposal in June 1989, it would pass to Clyde Coast.

JXN 341 was a Leyland Titan PD2/Park Royal H56R new to London Transport in December 1948 as their RTL21. It was sold to dealer Bird's of Stratford-upon-Avon in 1958 and resold to A1 Service member Ian Duff of Ardrossan in February of that year. It would remain in service until May 1966 and was resting at the company's stance at Parkhouse Road in Ardrossan. Clyde Coast member John Shields of Saltcoats then bought it and would run it for a further three years.

London came to the aid of A1 again when they sold off modern buses cheaply. OUC 46R was a Leyland Fleetline FE30AGR/MCW, delivered new to London Transport (DMS 2046) in October 1976. It passed to A1 member Andrew Hunter of Dreghorn in April 1983 and was taking on passengers at Irvine Cross. It lasted until 1989, when a new Leyland Olympian replaced it. It saw further service in Ayrshire on school contracts with Kerr's of Galston.

Dodd's persevered with the Seddon RU after others had tired of its faults, and added MXS 832L to its fleet in 1979. It had begun life with Graham's of Paisley (S2) in April 1973 and Dodd's would keep it in service until 1984. It was photographed at Dodd's Troon depot, located at Dundonald Road.

GSD 723V was the penultimate Leyland Fleetline FE30AGR/Alexander H78F bought new by Dodd's in June 1980, and is shown when still relatively new at Troon depot. It would have a short life with AA, being withdrawn in 1988 and sold to Leon of Finningley.

JSD 941F was a Leyland Atlantean PDR1/1/Northern Counties H78F purchased new by McKinnon of Kilmarnock in April 1968. It is seen entering the old A1 bus station, located in John Dickie Street, in its original livery.

SCS 384M was a Volvo B58-56/Duple Dominant C51F purchased new by T. & E. Docherty in July 1974 and is shown at the Bank Street depot in Irvine. It was later given A1 Service livery for use on the Glasgow Express Service.

JSJ 429W was a Volvo B58-56/Duple Dominant B53F, new to A1 Service member Tom Hunter in March 1981. On disposal it went to Wiles of Port Seton, then Rhodes of Yeadon, Yorkshire Rider (1461), Hylton Castle and Lancaster Bus. When new it had been painted in the livery of Graham's of Paisley, but was never owned by them.

B577 LPE was a Leyland Olympian ONTL11/2RSp/ECW CH45/28F, new in January 1985 to Alder Valley (1509). It passed to Clyde Coast in July 1991 and lasted just over a year. On withdrawal in August 1992 it passed to Cleveland Coaches (983) and was re-registered as PJI 4983. It must have liked Scotland, however, as it returned in July 1995, this time running for Stagecoach Western (911) until 1998. It was sold to Stephenson's of Rochford in 1999 and then to Tim's Travel of Sheerness in 2000. It was caught in Glasgow's Argyle Street on a commuter journey to Largs.

OSC 62V was a Volvo Ailsa B55-10/Alexander H79F new to Alexander (Fife) as their FRA62 in September 1979. It was already twenty years old when bought by Clyde Coast but would still give a couple of years' service on school contracts. It was working in Largs.

WAG 513K was a Leyland Leopard PSU3B/4R/Plaxton C53F purchased new in December by T. & E. Docherty of Irvine for their Cosy Ha' coach fleet. It later gained A1 Service livery for use on the Glasgow service and was sold to fellow A1 member Meney of Ardrossan in 1986. It was passing through Irvine while working on the Glasgow Express Service. It was sold to Clyde Coast Services in October 1988.

One operator's misfortune can be another operator's salvation. When Graham's of Paisley ceased trading in 1990, HGD 213T was bought by Steele's of Stevenston. It was a Leyland Atlantean AN68A/1R/Alexander H78F, delivered new to Graham's as their L13 in April 1979.

Dodd's worked under contract to Scottish Citylink and WSV 533 was used in Dodd's coach livery. It began life as ADV 143Y with Trathen's of Yelverton in 1982 and passed to Townsend-Thoresen Holidays. It joined Dodd's fleet when they bought the coaching side of the business in 1986, and was a Volvo B10M-61/Padane C49Ft.

The local service that connected Troon with Barrasie was actually licenced to Dodd's Coaches from 1953 to 1983, after which it became part of the AA buses network. It was operated by an AA bus but with a Dodd's driver. BND 874C was a Leyland Panther Cub/Park Royal B43D, new to Manchester Corporation in 1965, but had been sold off by 1971 due to reliability problems. It would last for nine years with Dodd's, although it must be said the operating conditions varied greatly from city work.

KXW 10 was a Leyland Titan 7RT/Metro-Cammell H56R new to London Transport as their RTL 660 in February 1950. It passed to A1 member James McKinnon of Kilmarnock in August 1966, and had the destination screen changed to McKinnon's 'Ribble' type screen.

Hutchison's of Overtown have long supplied operators with modern second-hand stock from their own fleet. E158 XHS was a Volvo B10M-56/Duple 300 Series B53F purchased new in January 1988. It was snapped up by A1 member Brown of Dreghorn in 1993 and was loading in Irvine.

Former Edinburgh buses are much sought after nowadays, but it wasn't always the case. GFS 410N was a Leyland Atlantean AN68/1R/Alexander H45/30D purchased new by Edinburgh Corporation in February 1975. It became an A1 bus in August 1992, when it joined the fleet of Steele's of Stevenston.

ENW 980D was the last front engine bus to join the AA fleet and seemed a strange choice for Dodd's. It was a former Leeds Corporation AEC Regent V/Roe H70R which arrived in 1976. It would remain for just over three years at Troon before sale for preservation.

A523 YSD proudly displays its Gardner badge and fitted in well with Dodd's mechanical preferences. It was a Leyland National NL116HLXCT/1R B52F bought new in May 1984 and is shown in Boswell Park bus station in Ayr.

Clyde Coast visited Edinburgh with RJI8 713. It was a Volvo B10M-62/Jonckheere C49Ft, bought new in February 1996. On disposal, the registration plate remained with Clyde Coast and the bus became N228 RGA with Hellyer's of Fareham.

CAG 619 was a Leyland Titan PD2/1 fitted with Leyland's own bodywork. It was purchased new by A1 Service member Murray of Saltcoats in 1948 and had a full life with the company, not being retired until May 1966. This view was taken at Parkhouse Bus stance in Ardrossan on a dreich day.

JKW 316W was a Leyland Atlantean AN68B/1R/Marshall H45/29D, new to South Yorkshire PTE as fleetnumber 1816 in February 1981. It was one of four purchased by W. Stewart of Stevenston in 1991–2. This one saw only two years of use with A1.

SRB 542 was a Bristol KSW6G/ECW H60R, new to Notts & Derby as their 314 in 1953. It was purchased by AA member Robert Tumilty of Irvine in February 1969 and passed to Dodd's when Robert retired in September 1972. It would last with Dodd's until April 1976, when it was sold to the Lincoln Preservation Group. It was coming out of Bank Street in Irvine as it headed to the railway station.

AML 88H was an AEC Swift 4MP2R/Park Royal B33D purchased new by London Transport as their SMS88 in April 1970. It was purchased by A1 Service member Docherty of Irvine in September 1977 and remained in the fleet until May 1990, although it was mainly used on schools and contracts. It has been captured working the Tesco contract as it climbs Chapelhill Mount in Ardrossan with the Firth of Clyde in the background. The bus was sold for preservation and achieved even more fame when Britbus made a model of it.

TSD 285 was a Leyland Titan PD3/2/Alexander H72F, purchased by A1 member Docherty of Irvine in March 1962. It is believed that it was originally ordered by Garelochhead Coach Services in 1959 but subsequently cancelled. It lay in primer, unused, at Alexanders' factory in Falkirk for almost three years. It ran until 1985 but remained in Docherty's ownership. It was re-registered to BHN 601B to allow the TSD 285 number to be placed on a new Volvo Citybus in 1985.

PAG 764H enters the new Kilmarnock bus station in 1977. It was a Daimler Fleetline CRG6LX/Alexander H75F, purchased new by James Murray of Saltcoats in March 1970. It passed to fellow member Robert Meney of Ardrossan when Murray sold his share on his retirement in 1982, but was withdrawn by October 1983.

BSD 560C was an AEC Reliance 2U3R/Duple Alpine Continental C51F purchased new by Dodd's in May 1965. It was sitting in Boswell Park bus station in Ayr. It was rebodied in May 1980 by Willowbrook and carried the prototype 003 body. It had been hoped to re-register it but this was refused; however, it received its cherished plate 5141LJ in 1983.

EAG 714D was the second of Dodd's Daimler Fleetlines new in February 1966. It would serve the company for fifteen years and was resting between runs on the Annbank service in Ayr's Boswell Park bus station.

XSD 789L was Scotland's first Leyland National. It had been delayed into service and its original number, XAG 637K, had to be voided. It joined the Young's fleet in September 1972 and was sitting at Ardrossan Terminus.

PJS 616L was a Ford R192/Willowbrook B52F, new to Newton's of Dingwall in November 1972. It passed to Clyde Coast member Kenny McGregor in May 1975 and lasted three years. The black roof was a remnant of its previous livery, but seemed to set it off. It was dropping off in Glasgow Street in Ardrossan, possibly on a journey from the ICI Ardeer Factory.

HCS 806V was a Volvo B58-56/Duple Dominant II C53F purchased new by McGregor in May 1980, and was preparing to go out on a private hire. On disposal, it would remain in Ayrshire, working for Shennan of Drongan and Liddell's of Auchenleck.

246 AJF was one of three ex-Leicester Leyland Titans placed in service by A1 in 1975. Its Metro-Cammell bodywork still looked good in this view taken in Irvine. It belonged to J. J. Stewart and lasted until August 1979, when it passed to Keenan of Coalhall.

East Lancs bodied Volvo Citybus demonstrator A308 RSU was tried by Docherty, Meney and Hill. It was loading in Irvine Town Centre and would in fact be purchased by A1 after its demonstration days were behind it. The livery included adverts by the Bus and Coach Council.

A308 RSU, seen as a fully fledged member of the Docherty A1 fleet, is passing Parkhouse Garage in Ardrossan. The bodywork had been modified after problems with the glazing. It passed to Stagecoach with the services and later saw service with Marshall's of Baillieston.

E76 RCS was a Scania N112CRB/East Lancs B51F purchased new by AA member Dodd's of Troon in November 1987. It would remain in service until the sale of the business to Stagecoach Western in June 1997, when it was allocated fleetnumber 451. It was nearing the end of its journey when it was photographed in Ayr.

OHS 979 was a Daimler CVG6/Massey H61R purchased new by McGill's of Barrhead in January 1960. It passed to A1 member James Brown of Dreghorn in January 1974 and was fitted with electrically operated platform doors before entry into service, and would run until 1978.

It was not uncommon for double deckers to reach Glasgow. F524 WSJ was an all-Leyland Olympian ONCL10/1RZ H78F purchased new by Hill of Stevenston in January 1989. Hill later traded as the Stevenston Motor Co., but went into partnership with Robert Paterson of Ardrossan in 1942 to form Hill & Paterson.

LVS 430P was an AEC Reliance 6U3ZR/Plaxton Supreme C53F purchased new by Limebourne of London in 1976. It was acquired by Duff of Ardrossan in November 1983, for use on the Glasgow service as well as private hire work. It had just arrived in Ardrossan on the express service from Glasgow.

Clyde Coast 'Soup-ercoach'! GNZ 9360 was new to Highland Heritage as R784 WSB and was on a visit to Edinburgh. The National Gallery was hosting an exhibition of the artist Andy Warhol and provided a surreal backdrop.

KTS 216H was a Daimler Fleetline SRG6LX-36/Alexander W Type B46D purchased new by Dundee Corporation (216) in March 1970. It passed to Tayside Regional Council in May 1975, but the bodywork was poor. It was re-bodied and re-registered as DSR132V by Marshall to B51F in April 1980 and sold to AA member Dodd's of Troon in March 1984. It would last until March 1989, when it passed to dealer Stevenson's of Uttoxeter and was resold to Nip-On Transport Services of St Helens.

EHJ 29X was a Scania BRH112DH/Marshall H78F, new in April 1980 as a demonstrator for SAAB-Scania. It ran for CIE in Eire as their DS1 (405UZ0) from new until April 1982. It went on loan to AA member Dodd's of Troon from December 1984 until actually purchased in June 1985. This view shows it in Irvine carrying an all-over advert for the Forum Shopping Centre. It was given a major rebuild in August 1990 using some Alexander body parts, which radically altered its appearance, and it finally received fleet livery at this time.

HRC 485D was a Daimler Fleetline CRG6LX/Alexander H77F new to Trent (485) in 1966. It was sold to dealer Ensign of Grays before joining the fleet of A1 Service member James Brown of Dreghorn in January 1979, mainly for use on schools contracts. It is seen in Saltcoats and it lasted in the fleet for three years. It must be said that it fitted very well into the A1 fleet at the time, but tended to be camera shy.

F149 XCS was an all-Leyland Olympian ONCL10/1RZ H78F purchased new by Ian Duff in December 1988. It had originally been registered F523WSJ due to an error and this had to be changed in January 1989.

JOV 765P was a Volvo Ailsa B55-10/Alexander AV Type H79F new to West Midlands PTE as their 4765 in February 1976. On withdrawal in June 1987, it passed to London Buses Limited as their V65. It later passed to London Northern before withdrawal in September 1990 and its sale to dealers Wombwell Diesels. It joined Clyde Coast in August 1993 for use on school contracts and remained until February 1997, when it passed to Liddell's of Auchenleck, becoming their No. 7.

Let's go back to June 1972 and see TCS 101 running along the coast at South Beach, heading for Ardrossan. It was a Leyland Titan PD2A/30/Northern Counties H64F purchased new by A1 Service member Murray of Saltcoats in January 1962. It would remain in service until August 1976, when it passed to Cunningham's Bus Service of Paisley as their No. 66.

F986 HGE was a Volvo B10M-60/Plaxton Paramount C53F new to Park's of Hamilton in March 1989. It lasted one season before disposal to Clyde Coast and was on a visit to Drumnadrochit, on the shores of Loch Ness. It would remain in the fleet until May 1992.

JOV 765P was a Volvo Ailsa B55-10/Alexander AV Type H79F, new to West Midlands PTE as their 4765 in February 1976. On withdrawal in June 1987 it passed to London Buses Limited as their V65. It joined Clyde Coast in August 1993 for use on school contracts and remained until February 1997, when it passed to Liddell's of Auchenleck, becoming their No. 7. Note the advert for Clyde Coast Self Drive.

WCS 843K was Daimler Fleetline CRL6/Alexander H78F new to Dodd's in May 1972. When new it was fitted with a Leyland Engine, which made it popular with the drivers, but this was later changed for a Gardner, which made it popular with the management. It was skirting round the coast at Ardrossan.

NAG 268G was one of a pair of AEC Reliance 6MU4R/Plaxton Elite C45Fs purchased new by Dodd's of Troon in April 1969. It was resting in Troon depot and would stay in the fleet until March 1982, when it passed to Quin of Ayr.

OSJ 37X was a very late-model Leyland Leopard PSU3G/4R fitted with Duple Dominant B53F bodywork. It was new to A1 member J. J. Stewart in April 1982 and it would remain in the fleet for six years. It would see further service with Wealden Beeline.

KAG 575 was a Leyland Titan PD2/20/Alexander H63RD, purchased new by AA member Young's of Ayr in April 1957. It was passing through Irvine on a local service and remained in service until 1976, when it was dismantled for spares.

PUF 631/TSD 630 were a pair of Guy Arab IVs, seen parked up in Troon Depot. PUF was new to Southdown in 1956 and joined Dodd's in May 1968, while TSD was purchased new in June 1962. Bodywork was by Park Royal and Northern Counties respectively.

LSJ 871W was a Leyland National NL116AL11/1R B52F, purchased new by Dodd's in April 1981. It was picking up a passenger at a deceptively quiet Irvine Cross.

KCS 179W was a Leyland National NL116L11/1R B48D, built as a development vehicle for Leyland in 1979. It was purchased in a hurry by John Hunter of Kilmarnock and sent back to Workington to have the centre doors removed. It wasn't a popular bus and was sold to Dodd's of Troon in November 1985. It only ran until August 1990, when it had to be withdrawn after an accident.

DCS 616 was a Daimler CVD6/Irvine C35F purchased new by A1 member Andrew Hunter in 1950. It was re-bodied by Massey as a double decker H61R in March 1958 and remained in service until 1976. It survives as an open-top preserved vehicle.

27 GWX was a Bedford VAL14/Willowbrook B54F new to A. & C. Wigmore of Dinnington in February 1964. On disposal, it passed to dealers Kirkby of Anston before AA member Dodd's of Troon purchased it in part exchange for SSD 326 in May 1967. It lasted for a very credible ten years in the fleet until April 1977, when it passed to contractor Muir of Kilmarnock.

EWY 76Y was a Leyland Olympian ONLXB/1R/Roe H76F, new to West Yorkshire PTE as their 5076 in March 1983. It was snapped up by Robert Meney in November 1986 and survived until the end of operations in January 1995, when Stagecoach took over.

C101 CUL was a Volvo Citybus B10M-50/Alexander H78D, new to London Buses as their C1 in August 1985. When new it was fitted with an experimental Cumulo drive system, but this had been removed prior to acquisition by McMenemy of Ardrossan in February 1988. It only remained in the fleet for one year before sale to Black Prince of Morley.

OSJ 607R was a Leyland Leopard PSU3C/3R/Alexander Y Type B53F new to Western SMT as fleetnumber L2607 in December 1976. It passed to Clydeside Scottish as their 607 in June 1985, then through various independents' hands until it joined Blue Bus of Horwich. It operated on hire to Clyde Coast before being formally purchased in September 1997.

PXI 5523 was a Leyland Tiger TRCTL11/3ARZA/Alexander (Belfast) C53F, new as Ulsterbus 523 in May 1990. It was one of a batch purchased by Dodd's in April 2008, seen working on rail replacement services from Glasgow Central Station.

FJ58 LSD was a Volvo B9R/Sunsundegui C53F, purchased new by Clyde Coast in August 2008, and was snapped on a private hire to Glasgow.

XSD 931L was a Ford R192/Willowbrook B52F purchased new by Clyde Coast member Hugh Frazer of Fairlie in August 1972. It was working on the Largs service when captured at South Beach, Ardrossan. It ran for a respectable seven years before sale to Jackson of Beith.

PAG 852H was a Dodd's Daimler Fleetline CRG 6LX/Alexander H74F, purchased new in March 1970, while HRC 487D was a similar bus, bought second-hand from Trent in February 1979. The location was Troon Depot.

PAG 762H was a Daimler Fleetline CRG6LX/Alexander H75F purchased new by Hill of Stevenston in March 1970. Hill's buses could often be identified by the silver star on the front panels. It was uplifting passengers at Irvine Cross and would serve the company until August 1981. It was then sold to fellow member J. C. Stewart of Stevenston and would give a further three years of service.

JXN 366 was a Leyland Titan 7RT/Park Royal H56R, bought new by London Transport as their RTL43 in January 1949. It was acquired by A1 member Docherty of Irvine in March 1958. In September 1963 it was converted to forward entrance H57F. It passed to fellow member Ian Duff in June 1971 and remained in service until November 1973, when it was bought by A1 Coachways of London.

TAG 699J was the last new bus purchased by AA member Robert Tumilty of Irvine before he retired. It was a Leyland Atlantean PDR1A/1/Northern Counties H70F, added to the fleet in March 1971. It introduced this new livery, for which Dodd's were very enthusiastic, but in practice it was hard to keep clean. Young's never adopted it and Dodd's quietly dropped it after painting about half a dozen buses in it.

TSD 630 was a Guy Arab IV 6LX/Northern Counties FH74F, purchased new by Dodd's in June 1962. It was a very reliable bus but hard work to drive on account of a very heavy clutch pedal. It remained in service until August 1977, when it passed to dealer North of Sheburn in part exchange for XGR 867, which was bought for spares and donated its engine to NSJ 381R.

LKP 381P was a Volvo Ailsa B55-10/Alexander H79F, purchased new by Maidstone & District as their 5381 in December 1975. It was one of a trial batch of five that the National Bus Company was testing. The whole batch worked for A1 at some time or other, but LKP 381P was acquired by T. & J. Hunter of Crosshouse in 1983 and ran for seven years. It was caught in Stevenston.

For a time, Clyde Coast extended the Largs-Saltcoats route into Irvine and MHD 336L was seen at the Cross. It was a Leyland National LN1151/2R B48D, new to Yorkshire Woollen (346) in November 1972. It worked for West Riding and Sheffield & District before joining Clyde Coast in June 1990, and it would last until sold to Arran Transport in July 1993. It passed to Western (L707) with that business in 1994.

C100 HSJ was a Scania N112DRB/East Lancs H80F purchased new by A1 Service member Brown of Dreghorn in January 1986. It passed to Stagecoach A1 Service with the business in 1995 and was later transferred to Hull. On disposal it worked for Robert's of Bagillt and Coachmasters of Rochdale.

PSJ 825R was a Volvo Ailsa B55-10/Van Hool McArdle H75D and was the last bus bought new by A1 Service member Tom Hunter in April 1977. It passed to son John Hunter in 1978 and lasted until October 1987, when it passed to T. & J. Hunter and ran until August 1990. It was converted to single door and luckily has been preserved in A1 livery.

GSU 841T was a Leyland Leopard PSU3C/3R/Alexander B53F new to Central SMT as fleetnumber T359 in April 1979. It passed through the hands of Kelvin Central Buses before sale to Inverclyde Transport in Greenock. Clyde Coast bought it in August 1994 and ran it for almost a year. It was running in service through Irvine when photographed.

Ex-Tayside Ailsas were an attractive buy for A1 and Docherty of Irvine took half a dozen. NSP 335R was passing through South Beach on its way to Parkhouse bus stance in Ardrossan. Docherty continued in business after the demise of A1 until 2008.

Dodd's purchased four ex-Tayside single deck Daimler Fleetlines in 1984. They had been re-bodied by Marshall in 1980, but only ran for four years before sale to AA Buses. This one was new as KTS 229H with Dundee Corporation. A nice touch was the fitting of a Daimler badge to the front panels.

YXD 507 was a Volvo B10M-60/Jonckheere C51Ft purchased in 2001. It had been new to Vale of Llangollen Tours in April 1992 as J459 HCA and was passing through Ayr to collect passengers for a tour to Pitlochry.

KSD 62W was a fine Leyland Atlantean AN68A/1R/Alexander H78F purchased new by John McMenemy in September 1980 and was taking fares at Irvine Cross. The McMenemy family operated from Central Garage in Ardrossan, which had previously been owned by Kerr & Linney.

CSL 605V was a Volvo Ailsa B55-10/Alexander H75D, new to Tayside (5) in February 1980. In 1996 it passed to former A1 member Hill of Stevenston, who had continued after the demise of A1 as the Stevenston Motor Co. Clyde Coast then acquired it for school contracts. It is seen running through Largs.

SF06 NBY was a Bova Magique XHD122 C49Ft, purchased new in April 2006 by Docherty. It looked good in the traditional 'Cosy Ha' livery, which had been inspired by the coaches of Webster's of Wigan, which became part of the Smiths/Shearings group.

TSD 630 was running empty through Saltcoats on a private hire and was a Guy Arab IV/ Northern Counties FH74F built to a style reminiscent of Southdown's 'Queen Marys', while a Western SMT Leyland Titan was picking up passengers outside the railway station.

UCS 763 was a Daimler Fleetline CRG6LX/Northern Counties H76F purchased new by A1 Service member Tom Hunter in 1962 and it is seen at Kilmarnock bus station. Sadly, on the night of 6 December 1979 OAG 761L was parked outside the garage of Tom Hunter, based at Crosshouse. In an act of vandalism it was set on fire and the flames quickly spread to the buildings, which contained other buses. GSD 366, a 1950 Daimler; Daimler Fleetlines CVG6/ TAG 60/WAG 709/OAG 761L; and Volvo Ailsas NCS23/4P were totally destroyed. UCS 763 and PAG 760H were badly damaged. The only remaining buses untouched were RAG 578 (now preserved) and ECS 57V. In true A1 fashion, services were maintained by borrowing buses from other members to work their share.

JHK 500N was a Leyland Atlantean AN68/1R/ECW H74F, new to Colchester Corporation in February 1975 as fleetnumber 60. It joined A1 in April 1989 when John Hunter of Kilmarnock put it into service, but it passed to Docherty of Irvine when they purchased John's share in November 1989. It was sitting at Irvine Cross while bound for Kilmarnock.

D573 LSJ was a Leyland Lynx LX112TL11 B51F purchased new by Young's in October 1986. It was seen in Irvine while bound for Ardrossan. It had been borrowed by Leyland Motors before delivery and demonstrated to a few operators.

ACS 42T was a Leyland Leopard PSU3E/4R/Plaxton Supreme C53F new to Clyde Coast member Kenny McGregor in April 1979. It lasted in the fleet until March 1987, when it was sold to Gibson's of Moffat, where it ran until May 1991.

G575 YTR was a Fiat 49.10/Phoenix B25F purchased new by A1 Service in July 1990. This was one of a pair delivered to enable the trial of minibus services in the area and these were the first buses owned by the company itself and not by individual members. The reason for this was to spread the risk evenly between all members. It was passing Parkhouse Garage in Ardrossan.

SOU 460 was a Dennis Loline I/East Lancs H68RD new to Aldershot & District (352) in June 1958. It was purchased by Robert Tumilty in August 1971 and passed to Dodd's when Robert retired and his share was split between Dodd's and Young's. This was Tumilty's depot at Gailes Garage in Shewalton Road in Irvine.

D29 BVV was a Fiat 49.10/Robin Hood B19F new as United Counties (29) in May 1987. It passed to Clyde Coast in 1994 and was caught in Kilmarnock while working the local service between Shortlees and Bellfield.

WCS 195 was an AEC Regent V 2D2RA/Strachans H63RD, purchased new by A1 members Hill & Paterson in 1963. Once again a silver star was carried, but another feature was the radiator stripes, which were unique to this member.

514 1LJ (BSD 560C) was an AEC Reliance 2U3R/Willowbrook 003 C53F caught resting at Troon depot. The chassis dated from 1965 but the body was only built in 1980 and replaced the original Duple Alpine Continental, which had become a little old fashioned looking.

EAG 980D was a Daimler Fleetline CRG6LX/Alexander H75F purchased new by James Murray in May 1966. It remained in service until March 1979 and was photographed in Saltcoats.

BPT 676L was a Leyland Leopard PSU3B/4R/Plaxton Derwent B55F, new to Trimdon Motor Services in July 1973. On disposal in February 1980, it was acquired by Graham's of Paisley (S19) then joined the Clyde Coast fleet of Kenny McGregor in April 1982. It lasted until 1986, when it went for scrap.

OKM 317 was an AEC Regent III/Saunders-Roe H56R built as a demonstrator in June 1949. It ran with Maidstone & District as their DH500 from December 1951 until 1952. On disposal it passed to AA Motor Services member Charles Law of Prestwick in 1952. When Charles retired from AA in 1953, it passed to Dodd's of Troon and, amazingly, remained in service until July 1979. It has been retained as a preserved vehicle ever since.

OCS 345L was a Leyland Atlantean AN68/2R/Roe H78D new to A1 Service member Docherty of Irvine in May 1973. It later passed to Kerr's of Galston for school contracts.

M151 FGB (M1ABO) was the last bus added to Docherty's A1 fleet. It was a Volvo B10B-58/Wright B51F, purchased new in November 1994 as M1ABO. This was a cherished plate and stood for Ayrshire Bus Owners. It was only to run for three months with A1 before Stagecoach assumed control, but was still to be seen in the area for many years after that in Stagecoach livery.

BND 875C was a Leyland Panther Cub PSRC1/1/Park Royal B43D, new to Manchester Corporation (75) in April 1965. It joined Dodd's AA fleet in March 1971 and lasted until September 1979, when it passed to a local contractor. It was looking very smart in this view taken at Troon depot.

MTF 665G was a Leyland Atlantean PDR2/1/Park Royal H79D new to Leyland Motors in October 1968 for use as a demonstrator, and it was exhibited at the 1968 Earls Court Motor Show. It was purchased by A1 Service members T. & E. Docherty of Irvine in February 1971 and was withdrawn in July 1983, passing to Skelmorlie Coaches. It was then purchased by Clyde Coast Services for spares in January 1989.

XAK 454T was a Leyland National 11351A/1R B52F new to Yorkshire Traction (454) in November 1978. It was added to the Clyde Coast fleet in December 1989 and stayed for four years. On disposal, it returned to Yorkshire and ran for Stringer of Pontefract.

1977 was the year of the Queen's Silver Jubilee and Dodd's repainted AML 629H to celebrate the occasion. It wore this livery from March 1977 until February 1978. It was an ex-London Transport AEC Merlin / MCW B50F, which had been new in 1969 and would serve with AA for four years.

Dodd's also served more exotic locations, as shown by E318 OPR. It was a Volvo B10M-61/Van Hool Alizee C53F, new to Excelsior of Bournemouth in April 1988, and was driving through Hamilton on Scottish Citylink 276, bound for Hull and connecting with the Zeebrugge ferry.

FSD 89V was a Leyland Leopard PSU3E/4R/Plaxton Supreme C53F, new to Hugh Frazer of Fairlie in March 1981, and was on a football hire to Glasgow. It was sold at the end of the 1984 season to the Stagecoach of Perth subsidiary in Edinburgh.

SCS 204J was a Seddon RU/Pennine B51F purchased new by Dodd's of Troon in January 1971. It was captured in Irvine in a very unusual version of AA livery. It was withdrawn in 1979 after an accident and dismantled for spares. The Seddon RU featured a Gardner 6HLX engine, which would have appealed to Dodd's.

AAG 312B was a unique bus as it was the only Daimler Fleetline ever bodied by Massey Bros of Wigan. It was new to A1 member Brown of Dreghorn in June 1964 and lasted until February 1979. This view shows it leaving the old A1 bus station in John Dickie Street in Kilmarnock.

ASD 888B was an AEC Regent V 2D2RA/Massey H63R, purchased new by Claude Dunn of Stevenston in November 1964. It would last until June 1979, but that was still in the future as it trundled round the coast at Ardrossan.

This coach, 1528RU (FHS 735X), had been new to Park's of Hamilton in April 1982 and was a Volvo B10M-61/Duple Goldliner C53F. It joined Clyde Coast in August 1993 and was working on the Glasgow service. This had been introduced in 1994 as a partial replacement for the A1 service, which had been withdrawn.

F747 XCS was a Leyland Olympian ONCL10/1RZ/Alexander H79F, supplied new to A1 member John McMenemy from dealer stock in February 1989. It was leaving Glasgow on the express service back to Ayrshire.

UWU 516 was a Leyland Titan PD3/5/Roe H61R purchased new by Severn of Dunscroft in June 1958. On disposal in June 1975 it was acquired by A1 Service member Steele's of Stevenston and would give around three years of service. It was photographed in Ardrossan on its way to Kilmarnock.

CCK 827 was an all-Leyland Titan PD2/3 H56R, new to Ribble as their fleetnumber 2655 in March 1949. It passed to Clyde Coast member William John Shields in June 1962 and ran until September 1966. It was scrapped in the Stevenston yard of A1 member J. C. Stewart by September 1967.

HSD 875N was a much later Clyde Coast vehicle. It was a Leyland Leopard PSU3B/4R/ Plaxton Elite C53F, purchased new by Hugh Frazer of Fairlie in April 1975. It was withdrawn in December 1989 and sold to Daglish of Kirkland, where it was re-registered as FSU 660.

E76 RCS was a Scania N112CRB/East Lancs B51F purchased new by AA member Dodd's of Troon in November 1987. It would remain in service until the sale of the business to Stagecoach Western in June 1997, when it was allocated fleet No. 451. It was waiting time at Irvine Cross.

TSO 24X was a Leyland
Olympian ONLXB/1R/ECW
H77F, new to Alexander
(Northern) as their NLO24
in March 1982. It passed to
Stagecoach before reaching
Clyde Coast in June 1999 and
was parked at Fairlie depot.

LFS 468 was a Leyland Titan
PD2/20/Metro-Cammell
H60R, new to Edinburgh
Corporation (468) in August
1954. It joined the fleet of J.
J. Stewart of Stevenston in
October 1970 and ran until
withdrawal in February
1974, after an accident cut its
career short.

CSD 199T was a Leyland
National 11351A/1R B52F
new to AA member Young's
of Ayr in July 1979. On
Young's retirement in April
1992 it became a Dodd's
vehicle, and was passing
through Burns Statue Square
in Ayr on a new service to
Ayr Hospital.

V9 DOT was a Scania K124/Irizar Century C51F, purchased new by Dodd's in February 2000. It was re-registered as V319 ESM on disposal to Ayrways in March 2006, and joined Mid Devon Coaches of Bow in August 2009 as YSU 895.

Clyde Coast registered local services in Kilmarnock from January 1994, after Handybus of Loans ceased operations, and this stepped up competition with Western. However, the entire network was taken off in September of that year. Western was by now a member of the Stagecoach empire and deregistered their competing Largs to Irvine service. Three Mercedes minibuses were sitting outside Kilmarnock's Palace Theatre at the end of their day's work.

ECS 56V charges up the hill at Saltcoats station on its way to Stevenston. It was a Volvo Ailsa B55-10/Alexander H79F, bought new by Docherty of Irvine in September 1979, and carries the usual heavy-duty bumper prevalent in this fleet.

PAG 852H was a Daimler Fleetline CRG6LX/Alexander H74F, purchased new by Dodd's in March 1970. It carries a broadside advert for the associated Dodd's television business as it edges out of Troon depot. It would remain in service until May 1984.

OHS 979 was one of a pair of Daimler CVG6/Massey H60Rs new to McGill's of Barrhead in January 1960. They passed to A1 Service member Brown of Dreghorn in December 1973 and lasted until 1978. OHS 979 is seen approaching Parkhouse Garage in Ardrossan and still looked immaculate.

After delivery of Dodd's last pair of Fleetlines, the company turned to the Dennis Dominator. This was the second one delivered in January 1982. It has to be said that the traditional livery looked well on the East Lancs bodywork as it uplifted passengers at Irvine Cross.

BCS 371C was the last traditional half-cab bought new by A1. It was a Leyland Titan PD2A/27 / Massey H65D, purchased new by John McMenemy in January 1965. It was sitting in Glasgow Street in Ardrossan in 1983 and would survive another year.

By the early 1980s, Clyde Coast were trying various paint schemes to modernise their image. One such attempt shows SSD 636M on a football hire to Glasgow. It was a Leyland Leopard PSU3B/4R/Plaxton Elite C51F, new to Frazer of Fairlie in May 1974.

McKinnon of Kilmarnock were the proud owners of ASD 29T. It was a Leyland Fleetline FE30AGR/ Alexander H78F, purchased new in April 1979, and its crew were taking a well-earned break at the Parkhouse Bus Stance in Ardrossan.

RSJ 656R was a Bedford YMT/Plaxton Supreme C53F, purchased new in June 1977, and it was on a visit to Edinburgh. It saw nine years of service in Dodd's coach fleet, which was very respectable for a lightweight chassis.

TAG 60 was exhibited at the 1961 Scottish Motor Show before delivery to Tom Hunter of Crosshouse. It was a Daimler Fleetline CRG6/Northern Counties H76F that was tragically destroyed by fire in a blaze at the operator's depot in 1979. It is shown in happier days, passing through Saltcoats.

C112 GSJ was a Leyland National 2 NL116HLXCT/1R B52F new to AA Motor Services member Young's of Ayr in November 1985 and it is seen loading at Saltcoats station. It would later pass to Dodd's of Troon when Young's retired in April 1992.

NTF 9 is an all-Leyland Titan PD2/15 H56R, originally built as a demonstrator for Leyland Vehicles in 1951. It has been in the ownership of A1 member Docherty of Irvine from December 1956 and ran in service until 1976. It has been preserved ever since and is still with the Docherty family as a reminder of the great days of Scottish buses, when passengers were given A1 SERVICE as standard.